FAMILY ISSUES AND YOU™

MOURNING A DEATH IN THE FAMILY

RITA KIDDE
AND ANTOINE WILSON

rosen publishing's
rosen central®
NEW YORK

Published in 2016 by The Rosen Publishing Group, Inc.
29 East 21st Street, New York, NY 10010

First Edition

Library of Congress Cataloging-in-Publication Data

Kidde, Rita, author.
Mourning a death in the family / Rita Kidde and Antoine Wilson. — First edition.
pages cm. — (Family issues and you)
Includes index.
ISBN 978-1-4994-3691-4 (library bound) — ISBN 978-1-4994-3689-1 (pbk.)
— ISBN 978-1-4994-3690-7 (6-pack)
1. Bereavement in children—Juvenile literature. 2. Grief in children—Juvenile literature. 3. Death—Juvenile literature. I. Wilson, Antoine. II. Title.
BF723.G75K53 2016
155.9'37083—dc23
2015017841

Manufactured in the United States of America

CONTENTS

INTRODUCTION

Dealing with the death of a family member can be very difficult. Someone who was once part of your own family isn't around anymore, and never will be again. The death of a close family member is hard to process and very painful to experience.

While a death in the family is never easy, everyone reacts to it differently. The shock of losing someone you love forever causes great sadness. But other feelings arise, too, and they can be confusing. People who have lost a family member may feel angry, guilty, lost, or even just numb. How you react to a loved one's death has to do with many factors, including your own personality, your experiences with death in the past, and how unexpected the death was.

Families are complicated things, and your relationship with the family member who died will also play a big part in how you react to that person's death. When someone you were very close to dies, it can be hard to imagine how you will go on without that person. It is also hard when a family member you weren't close to or didn't get along with dies. You may wish you knew the person better or appreciated him or her more. It's important to accept your own feelings about a family member's death. There's no right reaction to this kind of sad event.

Don't feel bad if you have trouble dealing with a family member's death. You're dealing with a huge loss, and it's understandable if you're not okay.

CHAPTER ONE

DEALING WITH DEATH

When someone close to you dies, you will go through a range of emotions. You will feel different things at different times. You may not feel sad the whole time. You may find yourself reacting oddly, with anger or with laughter. It is important to let yourself feel however you feel and to express your emotions honestly. In other words, if you try to put on a happy face for everyone or try to cry when you don't feel like crying, you will keep yourself from going through the natural process of grieving.

GRIEVING AS A FAMILY

Spending time together as a family can be helpful. After all, you are all probably missing the family member who died. Whether you are talking, sharing memories, or simply sitting together and crying, you can help each other cope with your loss.

However, you need to remember that every family contains a mix of personalities. Each family member will respond somewhat differently to a death. One of your parents might be open about his or her emotions, while the other keeps things inside. You might feel isolated and confused, while your sister is busy trying to take care of everyone else. Respect how everyone is

It often helps to talk about the relative who died with another family member. After all, the other members of your family are almost certainly missing the person who died, too.

feeling. Don't try to force others to experience emotions they are not feeling or to express their emotions in a particular way.

A family in mourning can be like a band in which everyone is playing a different song. Only by making a special effort to communicate can everyone understand each other. Family members often deal with death in different ways at different times. Be sensitive to how other family members feel, and listen to what they are saying about their feelings.

TALKING ABOUT DEATH

Communicating your feelings openly can help you during the grieving process. Keeping all of your feelings bottled up inside won't help you cope with the loss of a loved one. Let your family know that you are willing to talk about your feelings. Express your feelings as clearly and honestly as you can.

Parents and other adult family members may try to make death seem more pleasant by saying things like "she has passed on" or "he has gone on a long trip." They use these phrases to protect you from the reality of what has happened. If you feel that you can handle it, let your parents or other relatives know that you are willing to talk openly about death.

Your friends can be a source of comfort and support when a family member dies. Some people find it easier to talk to friends than to their own family members.

Some families are uncomfortable talking about death. If yours is one, you may feel more comfortable talking to friends. This is fine. Young people are often more willing to share their feelings when talking to other young people. However, your friends probably haven't had much experience coping with death. While they may provide a sympathetic ear, they might not know what to say. In any case, talking to friends can be a good way of sorting out what you're feeling. You can then share some of these talks with your family.

REMEMBERING A LOVED ONE ONLINE

Some families set up online memorials. These are websites on which people can write their memories about a person who has died or leave messages of support to the family members who remain. The sites often contain photos of the person who died and warm words about that person's life. Several companies host online memorials. Some are free, but others are not.

A person's social networking profile—his or her Facebook page, for example—often becomes an unofficial memorial after that person's death. If you contact Facebook, they will even turn the page of a person who died into an official memorial page.

COUNSELORS AND SPIRITUAL ADVISORS

If you are not comfortable talking about death and your feelings with your friends or parents, you may want to talk to a counselor at some point. Counselors have special training and can help you during the grieving process. Also, it might be easier to voice your doubts to a counselor, since he or she is not also grieving. For example, you might feel uncomfortable about the fact that you didn't cry at the funeral, but you don't want to talk to your family members about it because you don't want to make them feel bad. A counselor can help you come to terms with your feelings and behavior.

Speaking with a spiritual advisor, such as a priest, imam, pastor, or rabbi, may help you with some of the big questions, like "Why did this have to happen?" or "What comes after death?" Whether or not you belong to a religion or believe in a particular faith, spiritual advisors can provide comfort and wise counsel.

CHAPTER TWO

THE STAGES OF GRIEF

The most widely used model to describe the confusing, evolving reactions that people have to grief is probably five stages of grief. These stages were first sketched out by the psychiatrist Elisabeth Kübler-Ross in her 1969 book, *On Death and Dying*.

The stages are a tool for understanding the grieving process, not a map that needs to be followed. They don't need to be experienced in any particular order. People don't necessarily go through each of the five stages, either. Let yourself grieve at your own pace. When people try to rush themselves back to normal or keep their feelings bottled up inside, they can feel guilty or angry for years.

DENIAL, NUMBNESS, AND CONFUSION

Your first reaction to a sudden death might be: "It can't be true! I just saw him yesterday and he was fine." You may convince yourself that you're going to see this person again. This is called denial—when you refuse to accept the truth of a situation. A teen whose mother has died might find himself still waiting for her to come home from work at the end of the day.

When you hear the news that someone close to you has died, it may take a while for that information really to sink in.

Very ill patients, when they are told that they will probably die from their illness, often go through a stage of denial, too. They act as if they are not very ill, or not ill at all. They talk about what they're going to do when they leave the hospital.

To an outsider, denial might seem silly, even counterproductive. We may want to try to bring the person to his or her senses, to force the truth on the person. This is not a good idea. Denial is a normal reaction. It acts as a protective shield against unexpected or tragic events. Denial gives us time to adjust to bad news. Do not be ashamed or embarrassed to go through a period of denial after learning about the death of a loved one. You're not losing your grip on reality. You're just giving yourself time to adjust.

Numbness and confusion can also be early reactions to the death of a family member. Like denial, these reactions are most likely to come right after hearing that someone has died. Numbness is when you don't feel anything—when you feel detached from the world around you. Confusion comes when you seem to feel different things at once.

Both numbness and confusion are reactions to feeling overwhelmed. Numbness, like denial, can help us find enough emotional distance to begin to cope with our loss. If you feel numb or detached, don't try to force your feelings. They will come eventually, when your mind is more prepared to deal with them.

The best way to cope with emotional confusion is to talk to someone about what you're feeling. Don't be afraid to cry. Crying lets emotions out and can actually make you feel less confused. Holding in your feelings can leave you feeling very lonely. When someone close to us dies, we often feel isolated and alone, even if we're surrounded by others who love us and offer us support. Try your best to reach out to others so that you won't be alone with your pain.

ANGER

Once the reality of the death of a loved one begins to sink in, people often feel angry or frustrated. We feel powerless against death and lash out against those who we think hold power, such as doctors, hospitals, and parents.

When something bad happens, human beings naturally try to blame someone or something. Sometimes, this blaming process is appropriate. For example, we blame a murderer

A lot of people respond to the death of a loved one with anger. While it's not unusual to lash out at those around you, try to remember that they are not to blame for your family member's death.

for killing someone. At other times, we may end up blaming people who are innocent of any wrongdoing. For example, we might blame hospital nurses for the death of a sick relative. It's okay to express your anger and frustration. But if you blow up at someone who doesn't deserve it, apologize after you've cooled down. Let the person know that you're going through a difficult time. If some of your family members blow up at little things, try to understand that their anger may stem from their sadness or confusion.

GUILT AND REGRET

While the five stages of grief cover many of the common reactions to death, there are also other totally normal responses. One of these is guilt. When a family member dies, we might be left with guilty feelings: "Why did I live, when he had to die?" We might feel guilty about an argument we had with the deceased. We might feel regret that we didn't show more affection when he or she was still alive. Guilt and regret are normal parts of the grieving process. They don't mean you necessarily did anything wrong.

Communicating with your family about your guilt and regret will help you get these things off your chest. If you keep your guilt and regret to yourself, they will not just disappear.

BARGAINING

When a family member is dying, we might try to make a deal—perhaps with God or with the universe—to spare that person's life. For example, we might say to ourselves, "If he makes it through this surgery, I'll try harder in school" or "If she gets better, I'll devote my life to helping others." Usually, we don't share these bargains with others. An extreme form of bargaining for the life of a loved one is when we say, "Take me instead, and let her live"—offering our lives in exchange.

These imaginary bargains are another reaction to our powerlessness against death. It is an attempt to gain some control over something we don't want to have happen. This type of bargaining may be irrational, but it is a common reaction and one of which you don't need to feel ashamed.

DEPRESSION

Many people go through a period of depression when they are mourning the loss of a family member. When you are depressed, nothing seems worth doing. Depressed people tend to be tired and feel like they don't have much energy. Depression can make life seem hopeless and stir up feelings of helplessness, worthlessness, and guilt in a person. The specific symptoms of depression vary from person to person. Some people have trouble sleeping, while others spend a lot of their time sleeping. Some overeat, while others find they have lost their appetites.

As a normal stage of mourning, depression should not be ignored or rushed. However, if you find yourself heading deeper and deeper into depression—or if you feel that you've been depressed for too long—you should seek help. Talk to family

If the depression you feel after the death of a loved one continues at the same intense level for a long time, you might be suffering from complicated grief.

members or seek professional counseling. Eventually, as your depression falls away, piece by piece, you will begin to resume the routines of daily life, and your mood should improve.

ACCEPTANCE

After you have come to terms with your loss, you will feel like yourself again. You might have sad moments, but you'll be able to function more normally. Don't try to force yourself into this state of acceptance. Acceptance will come naturally, eventually. Time is the great healer.

When a dying person has accepted the possibility of his or her own death, he or she might wish to see fewer people, or even be alone. You should understand that this is a natural reaction to the situation. It does not mean that the dying person has rejected you or other family members.

CHAPTER THREE

WHEN A PET DIES

Many young people have their first personal encounters with death when a pet dies. Pets, especially those we are deeply attached to, can play an active and important role in our families. A pet's death can leave an empty place in our lives.

Even if you were not very close to the pet, others in your family might be feeling a great deal of pain. Respect the feelings of other family members. If you were close to the pet, you might find yourself thinking, "Why am I so sad? He was only a pet." Respect your own feelings. Don't hide your sadness. You have experienced a real loss, and you should be allowed to grieve.

PET FUNERALS

Consider doing something to honor your pet's memory. People often find it comforting to hold funerals for their pets. This can be a great opportunity to share happy memories about a pet's life. Keeping a framed photo of your pet around can be a comfort, too.

Whether or not you hold a funeral, you'll need to figure out where your pet's final resting place will be. Some people

It makes sense that we feel deep grief when our pets die. After all, many people consider their pets to be members of their families.

bury their pets in their backyards. However, this is against the law in some places. If you plan to bury your pet, make sure to check the laws in your town first. If burying a pet's body isn't legal, you might be allowed to have the pet cremated and bury the ashes.

People who have cremated a pet also sometimes choose to keep the pet's ashes in an urn in their homes. That way they can bring the ashes with them if they move. People looking for a permanent resting place for their beloved pets may want to consider a pet cemetery. However, this option can be quite expensive.

PUTTING A PET TO SLEEP

Jayden's cat, Smokey, was a good friend. Smokey liked to wait for Jayden to come home from school, and he always slept at the foot of Jayden's bed. Then Smokey got sick. Instead of leaping up to greet Jayden after school, he just lay there. Jayden and his dad took Smokey to

If your pet is in a lot of pain, putting it to sleep can be the most compassionate choice. After all, you will be sparing the pet a lot of suffering.

the vet, who told them Smokey was very ill and should be put to sleep. Jayden didn't want Smokey to die, but he didn't want Smokey to suffer anymore either. After Jayden's family put Smokey to sleep, they had him cremated and kept his ashes in a special urn in the house.

Sometimes, when a pet is very ill or has been badly hurt, the veterinarian (pet doctor) will suggest that he or she be "put to sleep" or "put down." Deciding to put a pet to sleep can be very difficult. It's a sad time, and the decision to put a pet down can make people feel guilty. If you have to put a pet down, remember that you are sparing it from suffering.

CHAPTER FOUR

LOSING A PARENT OR GRANDPARENT

Many kids or teens have experienced the death of a grandparent. If you were close to the grandparent who died, the experience can be very painful. As difficult as the death of a grandparent is, the death of a parent is generally even worse. On top having to deal with missing someone who will never come back, you'll need to figure out how the rest of the family works without your missing mother or father.

A GRANDPARENT'S DEATH

Your reaction to the death of a grandparent will probably depend on how close your relationship with that grandparent was. Because every relationship is different, everyone's experience of a grandparent's death varies. However, we can learn something from each example.

Diego's grandmother always took his side when he got into arguments with his parents. Sometimes Diego felt closer to her than he did to his mother or father. When Abuela died, Diego felt like he had lost the only person who could understand him. He felt alone and depressed.

If you were close to your grandfather—for example, if you lived with him or saw him every week—his death would cause big changes in your day-to-day life.

Diego's grandmother played an important role in the balance of their family, and her death left a gap in Diego's life. He had to learn how to connect with his parents in a new way. Sharing his feelings with his parents and expressing what Abuela had meant to him helped Diego develop a closer relationship with his mom and dad. The loss of one family member is an opportunity to develop a greater appreciation for those who remain.

Lily's grandfather wasn't able to move much or talk at all after he had a stroke. He moved in with Lily and her dad, who spent a lot of time caring for the elderly man. When Lily's dad told her that her grandfather had died, the first thing Lily felt was relief. Her dad would finally have time to pay attention to Lily, and Lily would be able to have friends over again. Her relief made Lily feel guilty, though.

ESTRANGED GRANDPARENTS

Some grandparents are estranged from their grandkids. This means that they do not have a relationship with each other, usually because some kind of disagreement. The disagreement may actually be between a kid's parents and grandparents. For example, your grandparents may not accept the fact that their son—your father—is gay or that their daughter—your mom—married someone from outside her own culture.

When an estranged grandparent dies, it can be hard to know how to feel. The grandparent was pretty much a stranger. It's okay if an estranged grandparent's death has little effect on you, just as it's okay if it makes you feel unexpectedly sad.

Though Lily loved her grandfather, he was also a burden. This complicated her reaction to his death. At first she felt guilty that she was more relieved than sad. After she talked to a counselor at her school, she came to understand that she had no reason to feel guilty. Your feelings are your feelings, and there is no right response to death.

A PARENT'S DEATH

The death of a parent is one of the most painful and difficult moments in anyone's life. It can bring about many different feelings, some of which can place extra stress on you and your family. When your mother or father dies, your family probably will be thrown into confusion for a period of time. The most important thing the surviving family members can do is communicate—talking or even crying with each other.

When Katelyn's mother died of lung cancer, Katelyn remembered all of the times she had hidden her mother's cigarettes. Now that her mother was gone, she kept thinking that she hadn't done enough to keep her mother from smoking. Even though everyone said that she shouldn't blame herself, Katelyn couldn't shake the feeling that she should have done more.

Like Katelyn, many people feel like there is something they could have done to prevent the death of a loved one. Usually, these feelings are irrational—they don't make any logical sense. But they are an important stage in the grieving process. By talking to her father and brother about these feelings, Katelyn found out that they, too, had felt similar regrets. This helped

A parent's death can be overwhelming, especially if it happens when you are still young. It's hard to imagine what the rest of your life will be like without your mom or dad.

her feel less isolated, and she was able to realize that she wasn't responsible for her mother's death.

> *Emily's mother was shot and killed in a hardware store parking lot by someone who wanted to steal her pickup truck. The would-be thief panicked and left the truck behind. He was never caught. Emily's life changed completely after that. She had a lot of feelings she couldn't express, but mostly she felt angry. She argued constantly with her brothers and couldn't concentrate at school.*

People aren't supposed to kill other people. But they do. And sometimes, they kill people they don't know, for stupid

TRYING TO UNDERSTAND VIOLENT DEATHS

Violent death can be extremely hard to cope with, especially when it happens in our immediate family. When someone dies of a disease, we might ask "Why?" but we will eventually understand that modern medicine still cannot cure all diseases. When someone dies in a car accident, we might be shocked by the suddenness of the death and by the tragedy of it. Still, we understand that car accidents are a part of modern life. However, when someone is murdered, understanding his or her death can be much more difficult, even impossible.

reasons. When those people are people we know, we are left with many questions and few answers. The man who killed Emily's mother killed her because he wanted to steal her truck. In the end, the killer never even took the vehicle. Emily's mother was killed for no reason at all. And, since her mom's murderer was never caught, Emily had no one to blame. This is an extremely difficult idea to accept. In a situation like this, it might be best for the surviving family members to seek the help of a counselor or pastor.

When Josh's dad died, his mother changed. She tried to put on a happy face for Josh and his little sister, but Josh could see how badly she was hurting inside. She lost interest in her work and spent much of her time in front of the television, looking dazed. Josh ended up having to cook dinner most nights. He started doing the laundry, cutting the grass, and taking out the trash.

After his father died, Josh immediately took on the role of caretaker. He set aside his own feelings to make sure that the people around him were okay. Inside, though, Josh was hurting. He distracted himself from his feelings by working harder. Eventually, he became depressed—he didn't feel like she had energy for anything.

Josh and his mother talked to their rabbi. She helped them see that Josh had avoided grieving for his father's death by caring for those around him. Josh finally began to mourn his father's death, instead of trying to replace him.

Jermaine's father died two months before Jermaine became the youngest-ever winner of a citywide chess tournament. Focusing on chess helped Jermaine cope

Taking on a lot of responsibility after a parent dies can make you feel a little more in control of your life. However, it can also be draining and a way to avoid dealing with your feelings of grief.

with his father's absence. After he won, though, Jermaine felt cheated that his father wasn't there to recognize his achievement.

Jermaine's frustration at having lost his father came from a deep anger at the unfairness of the world. "Why my father?" Jermaine asked. "Why now?" He looked around at all of the other boys who still had their fathers, and he felt cheated. It wasn't enough for his mother to be proud of him. She was always proud of him. He wanted to impress his father, who had always seemed distant. Jermaine expressed his feelings to his mother, and together they talked to a counselor. Eventually, Jermaine came to understand what lay behind his frustration and found a way to feel pride in his own achievements.

CHAPTER FIVE

LOSING A BROTHER OR SISTER

The death of a sibling (brother or sister) can have a powerful impact on a family. When someone dies young, it results in a heightened sense of anger and frustration in the survivors. The world seems unfair. Young people, we think, aren't supposed to die. When there is a lot of anger and frustration in a family, blame gets thrown around a lot more.

THE DEATH OF A SIBLING

No matter how you got along with your sibling, his or her death is a horrible thing to go through. If you were close, it may feel like losing a friend as well as a family member. If you didn't get along, your sibling's death may make you feel incredibly guilty.

Tyler and his sister had a big fight. Mia was older and had her driver's license, but she wouldn't drive Tyler to his friend's house. She wanted to hang out with her own friends. During their fight, Tyler said many mean things to his sister, and Mia left the house angry. That night, she was killed in a car accident. Tyler wanted to take back the mean things he had said. He wondered if the accident was his fault.

The death of a sibling is always difficult, whether or not the two of you got along. Making matters worse, your parents might be too upset to offer you much comfort.

Tyler never got a chance to take back any of the mean things that he said to his sister. This left him feeling very guilty after Mia's death. Tyler discussed this with his parents and found some ways to accept the fact that he could never speak to Mia again. His mother reminded him of all the nice things he had done for his sister, and that Mia knew that Tyler loved her. Tyler wrote a letter to Mia, apologizing for what he had said, which was buried with her. Tyler came to understand that the argument he had was minor, when looked at in the context of his entire relationship with Mia.

Natalia was the captain of the girls' soccer team. Everyone loved being around her. She was funny and had lots of energy. One day, Natalia killed herself. The whole school was in shock. Nobody could understand it. Natalia's sister, Ana, blamed herself for not noticing any warning signs. She told herself that she could have prevented her sister's suicide if only she had paid more attention.

Ana blamed herself for not noticing any warning signs. But Natalia didn't show any warning signs. She seemed happy with life. She hid her feelings behind a mask of happiness. A lot of people blame themselves for the suicide of a loved one. We scour our memories, searching for what we might have done to

COMMUNICATE, COMMUNICATE, COMMUNICATE

Your parents may have difficulty communicating their feelings, even with each other. You might hear that there is a very high divorce rate in families that have lost a child. This is a myth, or a piece of information that gets spread around but isn't true. The most important things are to keep the channels of communication open and to speak honestly about what you're feeling. Different family members will react differently at different times. Some, including you, might not feel like talking about the death. Be patient with your family and with yourself.

Your reaction to the death of a brother or sister will change over time. While you will probably have some of the emotional reactions outlined earlier in this book, more complicated emotions will arise, depending on the type of relationship you had with your brother or sister.

prevent this senseless death. Coping with the suicide of someone close to you will take time, but eventually your life will return to near-normal.

FAMILY TENSIONS

A child's death is very hard for the whole family. Having a sibling die doesn't just mean dealing with your own grief over the death. It also means dealing with the way the death has affected the other members of the family.

> *Dan's little brother, Ethan, drowned in a neighbor's pool. Dan's parents reacted to his brother's death in very different ways. Her father didn't want to talk about it. He spent longer hours at work. Her mother spent a lot of time looking at pictures of Ethan. Dan didn't know what to do. His parents weren't communicating.*

Dealing with the death of a brother or sister is painful to begin with. The tension that a child's death creates in the rest of the family makes it even worse.

Dan decided to approach his parents one at a time and try to talk about Ethan's death. Eventually, he was able to get his parents in the same room, and the three of them talked about how they felt. Both his mother and father confessed to blaming themselves for Ethan's death. When his parents understood that, in their isolation, they had been feeling the same thing, they felt relieved. It became easier for Dan to tell them how he was feeling, too.

Grace's little brother was diagnosed with leukemia and had to go to the hospital for chemotherapy treatments. His hair fell out, and, despite the treatments, he seemed to be getting worse. Grace asked her parents if her brother was going to die. They said that he would probably be fine. A week later, Grace's brother died. Grace was confused. Why didn't her parents tell her that her brother was going to die?

Grace's parents tried to hide the seriousness of her brother's illness from her. His death came as a shock to Grace, but her parents had been preparing themselves the whole time. Grace was angry that her parents had lied to her. She talked to a counselor who agreed that her parents should have told her what was going on. The counselor encouraged Grace to think about why her parents had decided to hide the truth from her. Grace spoke to her parents about it. They told her that they didn't want to scare her. She told them about how unprepared she had been for her brother's death and how angry she was. Her parents admitted that they should have told her sooner. Grace understood that her parents loved her and were trying to protect her. Her parents understood that they had made a mistake in not being frank with her about what was happening.

CHAPTER SIX

HONORING THE DEAD

There are a number of rituals that often happen after a person's death. For example, the person's family and friends may hold a funeral or a memorial service. Most funerals happen in a place of worship or in a funeral home. They usually take place quite soon after someone has died, and the remains of the person who died are generally present. This can mean a person's ashes in an urn or a body in a coffin or casket.

Memorial services tend to be less formal and are more likely to take place sometime after the person they honor has died. They are not likely to involve the deceased person's remains. Instead, they are a celebration of the life of the person who died.

Your family may not know whether you are ready to attend a funeral or memorial service. If you feel like you do want to go, let them know. If you feel too sad to go, try to help them understand how you feel. A funeral or memorial service is a great way to help you say good-bye to your loved one. However, if you can't or don't want to attend, that doesn't mean that you aren't mourning the death in your own way.

FUNERALS AND MEMORIAL SERVICES

Most funerals are led by a religious leader or a funeral director. Funerals follow a traditional structure, though what that structure is varies based on which tradition—especially which religious tradition—the person who died came from. Often, organ music is played and passages from religious texts are read. At many funerals, family members and close friends are given a chance to speak. If you think you want to speak at the funeral, talk to your parents beforehand.

Funerals are sad occasions, but a lot of people find them comforting as well. There is a finality to them, and they give people a chance to grieve together.

THE VIEWING

Sometimes, funerals include a viewing. This gives you an opportunity to see the body of your loved one for the last time. Usually, the body has been prepared for viewing, with makeup and dressed in a favorite suit or dress. Don't expect the body to look exactly like the person you knew. Viewing the body can help you realize that the person you knew is gone, and that his or her spirit is elsewhere. Talk with your family about whether or not you want to participate in the viewing.[/sidebar]

After the funeral, there may be a burial ceremony, in which the coffin or casket is laid into the earth at a cemetery or put into a vault at a mausoleum. This can be very emotional because it is so final. Sometimes bodies are cremated rather than buried. This means that they are burned and reduced to ash. The ashes of a loved one might then be buried, placed in a columbarium, or scattered over a favorite place, like the ocean.

Memorial services can be held anywhere. They are less likely to stick to the formal structures that traditional funerals follow. Written tributes to the person who died are common, as are readings and music. A variety of friends and family members may take turns sharing their memories of the deceased.

PERSONAL TRIBUTES

Consider creative ways to work through your grief. You may want to write down memories of the family member who died,

Looking at pictures of a loved one who has died is a great way to remember him or her. It's a perfect time to share stories about that person as well.

or make a collage or photo album to collect those memories. Maybe you can edit family movies to make a tribute. Doing this helps keep the memory of a loved one alive.

Creative activities—such as writing poetry, drawing, and painting—also help us explore how we feel. When they're shared with others, including our immediate family, we can communicate some of those deep feelings. You might want to keep a journal to help you understand what you're feeling.

RETURNING TO EVERYDAY LIFE

Returning to school after a death in the family can be very hard. At first you might find it difficult to concentrate in class. You'll probably have to make up work and you'll still be working through your grief. It will take time to adjust. Talk to your teachers and let them know what's going on. They will understand that you are going through a lot.

You will want to decide how—and if—you wish your classmates to learn about your loss. It can be embarrassing to have a teacher announce it to the class, so it may be best just to tell your friends what happened. However, your friends may not know how to react to the sad news. Some friends and classmates might avoid you, not because they don't like you anymore but because they don't know how to act in this situation. They don't want to make you hurt even more. A small effort on your part to make them feel comfortable will go a long way.

After time, your emotional pain will lessen. Some young people express a fear of forgetting their loved ones who have died. They worry that if they return to "life as usual," all traces of those who have died will be forgotten. But you can continue to live your life while also honoring those who have died. They can remain an inspiration to us throughout the rest of our lives. Their legacies can inspire us to do great things in their names. The things they have taught us will remain with us forever.

GLOSSARY

burden A heavy weight or load that needs to be carried.

cancer A disease in which abnormal cells grow uncontrolled, invading and destroying other parts of the body.

chemotherapy A treatment for cancer that uses chemicals or drugs.

columbarium A structure in which urns holding human ashes are placed.

cremation The process of burning a dead body and reducing it to ash.

deceased Died; a dead person may be known as "the deceased."

denial The refusal to accept the truth of a situation.

estranged Not close to, generally due to an argument.

funeral home A business that provides funeral services to the dead and their families.

grieving The sadness and other feelings brought on by a person's death.

irrational Behaving in a way that is not logical.

isolation Being alone or feeling alone.

leukemia A kind of cancer that affects the white blood cells.

mausoleum A stone building in which bodies of dead people are placed.

mourning Expressing grief or sorrow for someone who has died.

tribute An expression of respect, gratitude, or appreciation for someone.

FOR MORE INFORMATION

Bereaved Families of Ontario
Watline Postal Outlet
P.O. Box 10015
Mississauga, ON L4Z 4G5
http://www.bereavedfamilies.net/
This non-denominational volunteer organization offers support to families who have lost a loved one. They have affiliates in several different parts of the province.

Canadian Mental Health Association, National
1110-151 Slater Street
Ottawa, ON K1P 5H3
(613) 745-7750
http://www.cmha.ca/mental_health/grieving
Founded in 1918, this national charity helps Canadians deal with a wide array of mental health issues. The group's website has information on grief counseling and tips for dealing with the death of a friend or family member.

The Center for Complicated Grief
Columbia University School of Social Work
1255 Amsterdam Avenue
New York, NY 10027
(212) 851-2107
This center at Columbia University's School of Social Work was set up to study complicated grief, a form of long-lasting grief that takes over one's life. It carries out studies on the topic and can put those suffering from complicated grief in touch with the resources they need.

Centering Corporation
7230 Maple Street
Omaha, NE 68134
(402) 553-1200
Website: http://www.centering.org/
This organization publishes several magazines, including the quarterly *Grief Digest* and *Fire in My Heart*—a journal aimed at teenagers. It exists to help people who are in mourning get the resources they need to work through their grief.

Comfort Zone Camp
110 Meadowlands Parkway
Secaucus, NJ 07094
(201) 867-2077
Website: https://www.comfortzonecamp.org/
This group runs bereavement camps for kids aged seven to seventeen who have experienced the death of a parent or sibling. It provides a caring community in which kids and teens can deal with their grief. The group's Hello Grief website (http://www.hellogrief.org/) also provides an outlet for grieving young people.

The Compassionate Friends, Inc.
P.O. Box 3696
Oak Brook, IL 60522
(630) 990-0010
Website: http://www.compassionatefriends.org/
A group dedicated to helping families cope with the death of a child, The Compassionate Friends was founded by Chaplain Simon Stephens in England. In 1978, the organization made its way to the United States, where it now has more than 650 chapters.

GriefShare
P.O. Box 1739
Wake Forest, NC 27588
(800) 395-5755
Website: http://www.griefshare.org/
A ministry of the non-denominational Church Initiative, GriefShare has groups across Canada and the United States. These support groups meet weekly. At meetings, members watch videos, discuss with other group members, and share elements from their own personal studies.

The National Alliance for Grieving Children
900 SE Ocean Boulevard, Suite 130 D
Stuart, FL 34994
(866) 432-1542
Website: http://www.nationalallianceforgrievingchildren.org/
This national network provides resources to those hoping to help children and teens mourning the loss of somebody in their lives. It seeks to educate the public and holds an annual symposium on children's grief.

WEBSITES

Because of the changing nature of Internet links, Rosen Publishing has developed an online list of websites related to the subject of this book. This site is updated regularly. Please use this link to access the list:

http://www.rosenlinks.com/FIY/Death

FOR FURTHER READING

Bonanno, George. *The Other Side of Sadness: What the New Science of Bereavement Tells Us About Life After Loss*. New York, NY: Basic Books, 2010.

Goldblatt, Erica. *Grieving for the Sibling You Lost: A Teen's Guide to Coping with Grief and Finding Meaning After Loss*. Oakland, CA: Instant Help, 2015.

Hanson-Harding, Alexandra. *When a Friend or Loved One Dies: Grieving, Mourning, and Healing* (Helpline: Teen Issues and Answers). New York, NY: Rosen Classroom, 2013.

Hedtke, Lorraine. *Bereavement Support Groups: Breathing Life into Stories of the Dead*. Chagrin Falls, OH: Taos Institute Publications, 2012.

Helbert, Karla. *Finding Your Own Way to Grieve: A Creative Activity Workbook for Kids and Teens on the Autism Spectrum*. Philadelphia, PA: Jessica Kingsley Publishers, 2012.

Katz, Jon. *Going Home: Finding Peace When Pets Die*. New York, NY: Random House, 2011.

Kübler-Ross, Elisabeth. *On Death and Dying: What the Dying Have to Teach Doctors, Nurses, Clergy and Their Own Families*. Reprint ed. New York, NY: Scribner, 2014.

Lamm, Maurice. *The Jewish Way in Death and Mourning*. Revised ed. Flushing, NY: Jonathan David Publishers, Inc., 2012.

Marshall, Beth. *A Time To Heal: A Grief Journal*. Greenville, SC: Ambassador International, 2011.

Mueller, Scott. *What To Know Before You Go: An Insider's Answers to the Most Commonly Asked Questions about Death, Grief and Funerals*. St. Paul, MN: Mueller Memorial, 2015.

Paraclete Press. *Heaven Bound: Creating a Funeral or Memorial Service for Your Pet*. Orleans, MA: Paraclete Press, 2012.

Watkins, Christine. *Teen Suicide* (At Issue). Farmington Hills, MI: Greenhaven Press, 2014.

Wheeler, Jenny Lee. *Weird Is Normal When Teenagers Grieve.* Naples, FL: Quality of Life Publishing Company, 2010.

Wolfelt, Alan. *Finding the Words: How to Talk with Children and Teens about Death, Suicide, Homicide, Funerals, Cremation, and other End-of-Life Matters*. Fort Collins, CO: Companion Press, 2013.

Wright, H. Norman. *Experiencing the Loss of a Family Member: Discover the Path to Hope and Healing*. Bloomington, MN: Bethany House Publishers, 2013.

Yonker, Jennifer. *Thoughts of You: A Journal for Teens Coping with Grief*. CreateSpace Independent Publishing Platform, 2013.

INDEX

R

S

V

ABOUT THE AUTHORS

Rita Kidde wrote several of the titles in the *Jobs in My School* series for PowerKids Press. She lives in New Jersey with her family.

Antoine Wilson has authored books on economics and personal finance, presidential deaths, and the lives of literary figures. He lives in Southern California.

PHOTO CREDITS

Cover (figure) maxim ibragimov/Shutterstock.com; cover (background), p. 1 clockwise from top left Kzenon/Shutterstock.com, wavebreakmedia/Shutterstock.com, file404/Shutterstock.com, Antonio Guillem/Shutterstock.com; p. 3 sezer66/Shutterstock.com; pp. 4-5 Photodisc/Thinkstock; pp. 6, 11, 18, 22, 30, 35 Kzenon/Shutterstock.com; p. 7 Bruce Ayres/The Image Bank/Getty Images; p. 8 Jupiterimages/Photolibrary/Getty Images; p. 12 Fotokia/Photolibrary/Getty Images; p. 14 SW Productions/Photodisc/Getty Images; p. 17 JochenSchoenfeld/iStock/Thinkstock; p. 19 Tetra Images/Getty Images; p. 20 Dieter Spears/E+/Getty Images; p. 23 Ariel Skelley/Blend Images/Getty Images; p. 26 Tyler Marshall/Getty Images; p. 29 Ute Grabowsky/Photothek/Getty Images; p. 31 Lihee Avidan/Photonica World/Getty Images; p. 33 threerocksimages/Shutterstock.com; p. 36 Rich Legg/E+/Getty Images; p. 38 Jose Luis Pelaez Inc/Blend Images/Getty Images; cover and interior pages patterns and textures Irina_QQQ/Shutterstock.com, ilolab/Shutterstock.com, Cluckv/Shutterstock.com, phyZick/Shutterstock.com; back cover Anna-Julia/Shutterstock.com

Designer: Michael Moy; Editor: Amelie Von Zumbusch ;
Photo Researcher: Karen Huang